THE OPEN UNIVERSITY

Educational Studies
A Second Level Course

E200 CONTEMPORARY ISSUES IN EDUCATION

Block 2 The family as educator:
the childhood years

4 Mother-child interaction

Prepared by Will Swann for the Course Team

The Open University Press

The E200 Course Team

Joyce Barlow
Peter Barnes
Robert Bell
Eve Braley-Smith
Nick Brenton
Suzanne Campbell-Jones
Ronnie Carr
Chris Cuthbertson
Alex Finch
Ken Giles
Chris Gravell
John Greenwood
Tim Horton
Vince Houghton
Richard Hoyle
Audrey Lambart
Maggie Lawson
Kate Laughton
Ken Little
Fred Lockwood
Donald Mackinnon
John Miller
Ed Milner
Gill Norman
Sarah Reedy
Colin Riches
Peter Scrimshaw
Will Swann
Martin Woodhead
Peter Woods (chairman)
Ray Woolfe

Consultants

Aldwyn Cooper
Ronald Dore
Gerry Fowler
Bob Glaister
Andy Hargreaves
Desmond Nuttall
Ann Oakley
Kenneth Roberts
Nick Small
Peter Townsend
Leslie Wagner

The Open University Press
Walton Hall   Milton Keynes

First published 1981
Copyright © 1981 The Open University

Designed by the Graphic Design Group of the Open University.

Printed in Great Britain by
EYRE AND SPOTTISWOODE LIMITED
AT GROSVENOR PRESS PORTSMOUTH

ISBN 0 335 13003 8

This text forms part of an Open University course. The complete list of blocks and units in the course appears at the end of this text.

For general availability of supporting material referred to in this text please write to: Open University Educational Enterprises Ltd, 12 Cofferidge Close, Stony Stratford, Milton Keynes MK11 1BY.

Further information on Open University courses may be obtained from the Admissions Office, The Open University, P.O. Box 48, Walton Hall, Milton Keynes, MK7 6AB.

1.1

Contents

Aims

(a) To describe and analyse recent research in mother–child interaction;

(b) to use this topic as a vehicle for conveying some issues and problems of psychological investigation;

(c) to provide information on the educational role of parents to enable students to assess arguments about professionalism in education.

The first of these aims can be subdivided into three broad questions to which the unit provides some answers. These questions are given on p. 8. The topics considered in the unit are listed in the study guide. For the purposes of checking your progress, you may find it useful to look at the questions asked in my introductions to the readings and in the summary activities at the end of sections.

Note on reading

Set reading

The set readings for this unit are to be found in

REEDY, S. and WOODHEAD, M. (eds) (1980) *Family, Work and Education*, London, Hodder and Stoughton (Reader 1).

They are

SCHAFFER, H. R. (1977) 'Child rearing and early experience' (Reading 2.1).

SNOW, C. (1976) 'The language of the mother–child relationship' (Reading 2.5).

Further reading

BOWLBY, J. (1969) *Attachment and Loss: vol. 1 Attachment*, London, The Hogarth Press.

DUNN, J. (1977) *Distress and Comfort*, London, Fontana/Open Books.

RUTTER, M. (1972) *Maternal Deprivation Reassessed*, Harmondsworth, Penguin Education.

SCHAFFER, H. R. (1977) *Mothering*, London, Fontana/Open Books.

SCHAFFER, H. R. (ed) (1977) *Studies in Mother–Infant Interaction*, London, Academic Press.

SNOW, C. E. and FERGUSON, C. A. (1977) *Talking to Children: language input and acquisition*, Cambridge, Cambridge University Press.

STERN, D. (1977) *The First Relationship: infant and mother*, London, Fontana/Open Books.

Study guide

Time allocation

Unit component	Estimated level of difficulty[1]	Approximate study time hours	mins
Main text	2	4	30
Readings			
Schaffer (1977)	1		30
Snow (1976)	2	1	00
Activities			
1			5
2			15
3			15
4			10
5			5
6			5
7			10
8			5
9			10
10			10
11			10
12			10
13			10
14			20
15			10
16			20
17			5
18			10
19			5
20			15
21			15
22			20
Broadcast (including notes)		1	00
Assessment		1	00
Total		12	00

[1]Estimated level of difficulty: 1 = easy; 2 = moderate; 3 = difficult.

There are 22 activities scattered through this unit, forming an integral part of the text; therefore, unless you look at the comments on certain activities, the direction of the argument may not be clear. Several activities contain deliberately incorrect statements that you are asked to examine, and in a quick read through you may be misled by these.

I have tried to design the unit to allow you to cover all the major points in 10 to 12 hours, including a contribution to an assignment, but (if exhortation is in order) do treat the unit flexibly. There is scope for you to pursue further those topics that interest you most.

1 Introduction

1.1 Things never turn out exactly as you expect. I doubt if many people signing up for a course called *Contemporary Issues in Education* expect to find the fourth unit devoted to mother–child interaction. Yet it isn't too difficult to see that child-rearing is in some ways related to education. But what part does mother–child interaction play in education, and what has it to do with contemporary issues in education? Children learn a great deal before they go to school: they learn to talk and to understand many basic facts about our world. Because these things happen in nearly all children, and are apparently so effortless, there is a strong temptation to think that children do them more or less unaided. By contrast, reading, writing and arithmetic are achieved only with some visible effort and with the assistance of adults. This tends to make us take certain skills such as language for granted, although at the same time we have collective pangs of conscience about our children's reading standards. This is a very limited view of things: the truth is that children do not learn skills such as language on their own, nor is the process effortless. Parents contribute a great deal to their children's learning in the first few years, and there is considerable evidence that children who are not cared for early in life do not learn basic human abilities.

1.2 This has an important bearing on a key educational issue, one that is not just contemporary but has been with us ever since the advent of universal education: what claims do teachers have to their professional status? On what basis can they claim to be the best people to educate our children? What is the basis for teachers' claims to be important influences on children? Unit 6 will tackle these questions directly and, as a preparation for that, this unit will continue the task started in Unit 3 of examining what parents achieve with their children before school. This way you should be in a better position to examine the arguments about teachers' professional claims and the relative responsibilities of home and school in the education of children.

1.3 The approach in this unit is different in two ways from Unit 3. Firstly, I shall concentrate on the first few years of life: to the age of about three. Second, most of the material I shall discuss concerns children's and parents' *behaviour*, rather than their attitudes and beliefs. You will also probably find that the material in this unit is rather more removed from everyday common-sense ways of talking about children and their experiences. Nevertheless, because something is not immediately obvious does not mean that it is unimportant. Many subtle things occur when a mother and child come together: some happen so fast it is difficult to believe they could be influential, even if we could describe them adequately. I hope that this unit will show that these detailed behaviours that make up the relationship between a mother and her child can be described and studied by careful methods, and that the evidence that emerges is important in evaluating common-sense beliefs about the importance of mothers.

1.4 There are many questions we might ask about child-rearing, and, as with any subject, the more you study it the more questions are raised. What sorts of question can we tackle, and how?

Activity 1
Allow about five minutes

Here is a list of statements about children and child-rearing which embody some of the issues to be discussed in this and the next unit. Note down those that you agree with, disagree with, or can't decide about.

(a) Mothers should stay at home and care for their children until they go to school.

(b) Children are not harmed at all by being cared for in day nurseries.

(c) Children develop a deep-seated emotional bond with their mothers that is quite unlike any other relationship.

(d) A deprived child turns into a deprived adult.

(e) Mothers determine when and how a baby is fed.

(f) When a baby cries persistently, if you ignore it, it will stop eventually.

(g) Soothing irritable babies makes them spoilt later on.

(h) Parents' baby-talk does not help children to learn language any faster.

(j) Very young babies in the first ten weeks of life are incapable of any organized behaviour apart from crying, feeding and excreting.

Which of these claims could be checked with facts; which involve values or elements of both fact and value? If you are in doubt about the distinction between these categories, refresh your memory by reading Unit 2, 2.1 to 2.5.

Comment

(a) The only statement that is unambiguously a value judgement and nothing else.

(b) This is an empirical claim, but it can only be answered if we know what 'harmed' means, and this involves a value judgement.

(c) A question of fact.

(d) Like statement (b), but even more slippery because 'deprived' is used in two distinct senses: withdrawal of stimulation, support or love from the child and the absence of certain psychological characteristics in the adult. Both can be empirically identified, both have value-laden overtones.

(e)–(j) Questions of fact.

1.5 As you can see, common-sense statements about child-rearing very often mix up matters of fact and value. In this unit we shall be looking only at factual questions, but they are all questions that have a bearing on value judgements about child-rearing. Even so, I shall not be offering any very straightforward answers, because the questions themselves are never very straightforward. Take statement (g) in Activity 1. In order to decide whether this is true or not, we would need to:

(i) Say what 'soothing' meant. What behaviours count as soothing?

(ii) Identify when babies are irritable. What counts as irritable? What behaviours indicate irritability? How intense must they be to count as indications of irritability?

(iii) Observe the effects of soothing on babies when irritable and quiet.

(iv) State precisely what we mean by 'spoilt'.

(v) Study the children later on to see if they become spoilt, and whether they go on being spoilt.

All this would only amount to the start of what would be a very complex study. In order to understand and assess the results, we would need to know how these various problems of method were resolved; otherwise we might misinterpret the results, because, for example, what *we* meant by 'soothing' or 'irritable' was not what the investigator meant. So methods and results are very closely related, and I shall be spending some time looking at methods of study in a number of experiments.

1.6 We begin our investigation into the importance of mothers by examining children who are deprived of normal child-rearing. Are such children handicapped as a result of this experience? If they are, then can we conclude that mothers are important? Here we are studying the mother's influence much as we might study the effects of plant food on plants, i.e. by depriving some plants and feeding others. We shall separate two areas of development in which mothers may be important: emotional and intellectual. Then we shall look in turn at these two kinds of development and we shall find that they have certain links. Our examination of intellectual development will be largely restricted to language and communication. Throughout all this, we shall be concentrating on three kinds of questions:

(a) What sorts of things do mothers do with their children?

(b) How do children's developing skills and abilities affect the ways they are treated by their mothers?

(c) What are the immediate consequences of mothers' behaviour for their children's development?

1.7 You may have detected a peculiar prejudice in my discussion: why do I only refer to mothers? The problem is tricky; most research has been with mothers, or female substitutes, and it cannot be assumed that findings apply equally to fathers, or indeed to caretakers in general. This partly reflects the experience of the majority of children, for whom the mother is the primary caretaker; to a degree, it also reflects the perceptions of research workers. However, studies of the father's role have revealed, not surprisingly, that he can play a very important part in the child's development, and this is sometimes important in answering questions such as whether or not a child must be reared by a woman. So most of the time I shall refer to mothers, only for reasons of accuracy, and bring in fathers and other relatives where there is pertinent evidence.

2 Maternal deprivation

2.1 One way to study the importance of mothers is to examine cases of children who have not had normal contact with them and who have been placed in institutions. Such children were the focus of a number of studies in various parts of the world in the late forties and early fifties. In 1953, John Bowlby, an English psychiatrist, presented a very influential thesis which drew upon much of this research. Here is a summary of his view of the area as it was then:

> Among the most significant developments of psychiatry during the past quarter of a century has been the steady growth of evidence that the quality of the parental care which a child receives in his earliest years is of vital importance for his future mental health.
>
> Largely as a result of this new knowledge, there is today a high level of agreement among child-guidance workers in Europe and America on certain central notions. These workers are alike in the way in which they approach and study and diagnose their patients, in the aims of their treatments, and above all in the theories of the causes of mental ill-health on which their work is founded . . . For the moment it is sufficient to say that what is believed to be essential for mental health is that an infant and young child should experience a warm, intimate and continuous relationship with his mother (or permanent mother-substitute—one person who steadily 'mothers' him) in which both find satisfaction and enjoyment. It is this complex, rich, and rewarding relationship with the mother in early years, varied in countless ways by relations with the father and with the brothers and sisters, that child psychiatrists and many others now believe to underlie the development of character and of mental health.
>
> A state of affairs in which a child does not have this relationship is termed 'maternal deprivation'. This is a general term covering a number of different situations. Thus, a child is deprived even though living at home if his mother (or permanent mother-substitute) is unable to give him the loving care small children need. Again, a child is deprived if for any reason he is removed from his mother's care. This deprivation will be relatively mild if he is then looked after by someone whom he has already learned to know and trust, but may be considerable if the foster-mother even though loving is a stranger. All these arrangements, however, give a child some satisfaction and are therefore examples of 'partial deprivation'. They stand in contrast to the almost 'complete deprivation' which is still not uncommon in institutions, residential nurseries, and hospitals, where a child often has no one person who cares for him in a personal way and with whom he may feel secure.
>
> The ill-effects of deprivation vary with its degree. Partial deprivation brings in its train anxiety, excessive need for love, powerful feelings of revenge, and, arising from these last, guilt and depression. A young child, still immature in mind and body, cannot cope with all these emotions and drives. The ways in which he responds to these disturbances of his inner life may in the end bring about nervous disorders and instability of character. Complete deprivation . . . has even more far-reaching effects on character development and may entirely cripple the capacity to make relationships with other people. Many workers have investigated the connexion between 'broken homes' and the failure of children to adjust themselves to life with other people. But though these studies have confirmed the far-reaching importance of a child's early experience of home, the idea of a 'broken home' brings in too many varied conditions to be a satisfactory classification for scientific study; it is better to fix our minds on the child's developing relationship with his mother and father. When we do this, much that was obscure in the origins of mental illness becomes clear . . .
>
> Evidence that the deprivation of mother-love in early childhood can have a far-reaching effect on the mental health and personality development of human beings comes from many sources . . . They make it plain that, when deprived of maternal care, a child's development is almost always retarded—physically, intellectually, and socially—and that symptoms of physical and mental illness may appear. Such evidence is disquieting, but sceptics may question whether the check is permanent and whether the symptoms of illness may not easily be overcome. The retrospective and follow-up studies make it clear that such optimism is not always justified and that some children are gravely damaged for life. This is a sombre conclusion, which must now be regarded as established.
>
> (Bowlby, J., 1953, pp. 13–22)

2.2 If it is the case that without a mother's continuous warm care a child's personality and intelligence is damaged, then we would have clear evidence that mothers play a vital role in children's development. Bowlby was so convinced that this was true that he said that a bad home was often better for a child than a good institution. At the same time a report of the World Health Organization, which sponsored Bowlby's work, stated that day nurseries could lead to 'permanent damage to the emotional health of a future generation' (WHO, 1951) and later it was claimed that 'anything that hinders women in the fulfilment of this mission [full-time child-rearing] must be regarded as contrary to human progress' (Baers, 1954). These ideas had considerable influence on social policy and day-to-day child care practice; they led, for example, to a marked reluctance by some local authorities to take children into care, when the home circumstances were nothing short of appalling.

2.3 As evidence in support of his claims Bowlby presented studies of children reared in long-stay institutions whose development had been followed over a long period. In one such study Goldfarb (1955) investigated the development of 30 children up to the ages of ten to fourteen. Half these children were placed in an institution at the age of six months, stayed until they were three and a half years old and were then transferred to foster homes; the other half went straight into foster homes at six months. When these children were examined in early adolescence, the first group were found to score lower than the second on measures of intelligence, language, academic achievement and social maturity.

Activity 3
Allow about 15 minutes

Bowlby takes this as evidence for his claims about the effects of maternal deprivation. But from the description of the experiment I have given you can you conclude that institutional rearing caused later deficits? Of the following points, which might alter that conclusion, and how? Do these points show up faults in the design of the study? Do they offer evidence that conflicts directly with Goldfarb's claim, or do they extend and refine his claim?

(a) Goldfarb does not say how children were selected for early fostering.

(b) At three and a half years the two groups of children were already different in their abilities.

(c) Other studies of a similar kind have failed to find any intellectual, social or emotional deficits in institution-reared children.

(d) Certain changes in the quality of care provided in institutions lead to improvements in children's intellectual level.

(e) The longer a child remains in an institution that does have adverse effects, the more intellectual deficit and emotional disturbance she or he is likely to show.

(f) Many cases show that a complete and positive change of environment for institutionalized or otherwise deprived children leads to a reversal of intellectual and emotional difficulties.

Comment

(a) It is possible that certain kinds of children were systematically creamed off for early fostering. Apart from the possible effects of early cognitive ability, it is known that some types of children react more adversely to family stress than others.

(b) This does not affect the conclusion about long-term effects.

(c) Obviously many different factors could determine the differences between Goldfarb's and others' results: the children used, their social background, the age they were placed in an institution and, most obviously, the *quality of care* provided by that institution.

(d) Here is stronger evidence that quality of care is an important factor in determining children's development.

(e) Because the length of maternal deprivation affects the outcome, we should take care in generalizing from stays of three years to stays of less time. You could now look at how studies of permanent separation, such as Goldfarb's, could possibly offer support for the statements made by Baers and the World Health Organization.

(f) This modifies any claim that the effects of institution-rearing are permanent. Note that Goldfarb only studied the children up to the ages of 10–14.

2.4 Studying children placed in institutions in order to establish the importance of the mother–child relationship is fraught with difficulties. We can see from Activity 3 that several factors can affect a child's responses to maternal deprivation. First, there is the kind of deprivation experienced, which might range from the merest transient loss when mother leaves the room, through daily separation from working mothers (an issue discussed in Unit 5), to total and permanent separation. Second, a very important factor is the kind of care provided in the institution, and this can often provide very useful pointers to those features of maternal care that are important, as we shall see shortly. Third, responses to severe deprivation need not be permanent if a marked improvement in the environment occurs.

2.5 In addition, we need to take into account the kinds of behaviour or ability affected by the adverse conditions. The early studies surveyed by Bowlby found two distinct effects of rearing in the institutions studied: a particular *emotional* reaction to separation, and *intellectual* retardation.

2.6 The short-term emotional reactions of most, though not all, children separated from their mothers follow three phases: an initial period of *protest*, in which the child is acutely distressed and cries a great deal; a period of *despair*, when the child becomes apathetic and quietly morose; a period of *detachment*, when children lose interest in their parents. (The terms are those used by Robertson and Bowlby, 1952.) Later on, Bowlby found that children reared in institutions developed a number of unusual characteristics: the formation of indiscriminate and superficial friendships, an inability to form emotionally close bonds with others, antisocial behaviour, depression—a whole array of emotional and social difficulties. He argued, therefore, that a stable, enduring and continuous loving relationship with the mother was necessary for children's emotional development.

2.7 Investigations over the past 25 years have both modified Bowlby's claims and increased our knowledge of the important features of the mother–child relationship. Bowlby himself has played an important part in this reappraisal (see Bowlby, 1969).

Activity 4
Allow about ten minutes

Here is some of the evidence about the short-term emotional effects of separation gathered during the past 25 years:

(a) Children under the age of six months do not usually show any emotional reactions.

(b) Children are much less distressed when separated from their mother if they have a brother or sister with them.

(c) Children placed in hospitals where their mothers can visit them daily also show distress reactions, though these are much less marked than when visiting is not possible.

(d) Children are less distressed in hospital if they have toys to play with (when their mothers are present).

(e) Children are less distressed when the people who care for them during separation are not complete strangers.

We know from Activity 3 that several factors are involved in a child's response to separation. What can you conclude about these factors from the evidence outlined above, and in what ways does this evidence extend and refine Bowlby's claims?

Comment

(a) This suggests that some fairly important change takes place in the emotional development of children at around six months. If children are not upset by separation until six months of age, does this mean that they are indiscriminate in their affections for the first six months? This is discussed in Section 3.

(b) Mothers are not the only people who matter to children. If siblings help reduce distress in similar ways to mothers, then the emotional relationship of child to sibling may share common features with the mother–child relationship.

(c) The extent of separation is an important factor in modifying distress reactions.

(d) Certain features of the physical environment appear to relieve distress. Why and how this happens is not clear, nor is it clear what kinds of toys might play a role in this. Toys may help to reduce the strangeness of the new environment.

(e) See comment (b) above.

2.8 It appears that immediate reactions to separation are modified by the degree of familiarity with the new environment and the degree of continuity between home and hospital. Any claim that mothers play the key role in their child's emotional development to the exclusion of all else is not supported by the evidence available. In Section 3, we shall look at studies of normal emotional development to learn more directly about its nature.

2.9 Not only did Bowlby find emotional difficulties to be a result of rearing in institutions; he also found intellectual retardation. Again, a closer study of the factors determining and modifying this retardation may provide useful pointers to discovering what role mothers normally play in their children's intellectual development. A good example of the evidence available is a study by Sayegh and Dennis (1965), who looked at a group of 13 orphans between the ages of seven and 18 months in a residential nursery. At the start of this study the children's development was assessed on the Cattell Infant Intelligence Scale. (This test of intelligence, devised for children aged 2–30 months, comprises some standard IQ items measuring children's responses to specific tasks and other items based on naturalistic observations of the child's development.) The development of the children studied was found to be between the average two-month-old's level and the average eight-month-old's level. Figure 1 shows the relationship between the children's age and their 'developmental age', i.e. the level of cognitive development they had reached. It is clear that the institution-reared children's development is considerably slower, and that the older these children are the more retarded they are compared to their normal peers.

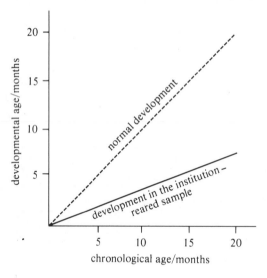

Figure 1 *Chronological and developmental age in a group of institution-reared children (adapted from Sayegh and Dennis, 1965).*

2.10 Some of the sources of retardation are illustrated by a study by Dennis (1960) who compared three institutions for orphans in Iran. He found that in two of the institutions children were markedly more retarded, and also that in these two the children lacked toys, play opportunities and were handled less. Some further evidence bearing on the sources of retardation in institutions is:

(i) Retardation is evident from as early as two months.

(ii) Daily tactile stimulation for as little as 20 minutes per day over ten weeks leads to higher levels of intellectual ability in infants.

(iii) Extra individual communication and attention by staff leads to greater social responsiveness in institution-reared infants.

(iv) Providing toys with which infants and adults can play together leads to a higher rate of intellectual development in institutionalized infants than in those not given this experience.

Activity 5
Allow about five minutes

Which of the following statements are supported by the evidence presented above?

(a) Intellectual and emotional effects of institutional child-rearing have similar causes (look also at Activity 4).

(b) Extra stimulation improves the development of institution-reared infants.

(c) Tactile stimulation is more important than verbal stimulation for infants' intellectual development.

Comment   None of these statements can be safely concluded from the evidence given in paragraph 2.10.

(a) If you compare this evidence with that given in paragraphs 2.6 to 2.8 you will see that the timing of the emergence of emotional and intellectual reactions is different. This strongly suggests different underlying causes.

(b) This is too broad a statement. The evidence shows the effects of a particular kind of stimulation.

(c) Nothing in the evidence allows any conclusions about the relative importance of different forms of stimulation.

2.11   Many other results confirm the finding that intellectual development is in large part determined by the quality of a child's environment, and in Sections 4 and 5 we shall look more closely at the nature of the normal environment a child experiences and its role in development.

Summary

2.12   We have looked at some studies that have tried to investigate the importance of the mother–child relationship by examining cases where it is disrupted; because human experience is rarely straightforward, the early conclusions have had to be modified.

2.13   Bowlby's theory divides into three interrelated issues:

(a) The claim that the mother–child relationship provides something without which children cannot develop normally.

(b) The claim that institutions cannot provide a complete substitute for a child's mother.

(c) The claim that the effects of early experiences cannot readily be reversed in later life.

2.14   The second of these issues will be discussed further in Unit 5, particularly that side of the debate concerned with working mothers and the provision of day care. The third issue is discussed in the reading by Schaffer (Reading 2.1 in Reader 1); it represents a current area of great interest in developmental psychology and although there is not space to deal with it here in any depth you might later on study E201, *Personality and Learning* (The Open University, 1976) , or E362, *Cognitive Development* (The Open University, 1979), both of which deal with this issue. The first issue is our topic for the remainder of this unit.

Reading   You have already read H. R. Schaffer, 'Child rearing and early experience' (Reading 2.1 in Reader 1). There are several questions that you may find useful in refreshing your memory:

(a) How important is the physical care of a child for his later personality development?

(b) How satisfactory a method of study is asking parents about their child-rearing practices?

(c) How important are the early years of life in shaping personality?

(d) What problems occur in studying the effects of early experience?

3 Emotional development and attachment

The nature of attachment

3.1 One important feature of children's early emotional life is the close relationships they establish with the people round about them. It was the disruption of these relationships that concerned Bowlby. One part of such relationships, particularly that with the mother, has been called attachment. An attachment, in the words of Ainsworth and Bell (1970), is:

> . . . an affectional tie that one person or animal forms between himself and another specific one—a tie that binds them together in space and endures over time. The behavioral hallmark of attachment is seeking to gain and to maintain a certain degree of proximity to the object of attachment . . .

> (Ainsworth and Bell, 1970, p. 50)

3.2 Children develop such specific emotional bonds to the adults in their lives, which they do not develop towards strangers; so, for example, in the second half of the first year a child's attachment-figure is better at stopping the child crying, and at the same period children often react to separation from their attachment-figures by crying, fussing or following them around.

3.3 Attachment is not simply an interesting process in early childhood; it has been claimed on the basis of studies of monkeys (Harlow and Harlow, 1969) and humans (Bowlby, 1969) that the formation of specific attachments is vital for a child's later emotional and social well-being.

3.4 Three kinds of behaviours have been used to identify and measure attachments:
   (a) Behaviours that promote and maintain contact with the attachment-figure. This can be either direct physical contact or through sight and hearing.
   (b) Reactions to separation from the attachment-figure. The range of types of separation that have been studied is enormous, from putting a child down after holding him to total separation as a result of the parents' death.
   (c) Reactions to strangers and strange environments, and the importance of the attachment-figure in modifying these reactions.

Activity 6
Allow about five minutes

Which infant behaviours would you look for if you wanted to measure attachment? Note down some likely candidates which fall into the categories in paragraph 3.4.

3.5 Mary Ainsworth, in a study of children of the Ganda tribe of Uganda, catalogued 13 behaviour patterns which she said indicated attachment (Ainsworth, 1964). Looking through her list below, you will see that the three categories in paragraph 3.4 are not mutually exclusive: children are often separated from mothers and thereby put into strange environments; many of the reactions to separation are behaviours that promote contact with the mother.

Patterns of attachment behaviour

1 *Differential crying* The baby cries when held by someone other than the mother, and stops when taken by the mother.
2 *Differential smiling* The baby smiles more readily and more often at his mother than at others.
3 *Differential vocalization* The baby vocalizes more readily and more often to his mother than to others.
4 *Visual-motor orientation* The baby keeps his eyes more or less continuously on his mother when physically separated but able to see her.
5 *Crying on separation* The baby cries when the mother leaves his sight.
6 *Following* When the baby can crawl or walk, he follows his mother when she leaves his sight.
7 *Scrambling* The baby climbs over his mother, explores her, plays with her face, hair and clothes.
8 *Burying the face* Returning to the mother, the baby buries his face in her lap.

9 *Exploration from a secure base* When the baby can crawl, he will make forays away from his mother to explore the close environment. He is much less likely to do this when his mother is not present, and reacts with distress if she moves off while he is exploring.

10 *Clinging* This happens particularly in response to the presence of strangers or frightening objects.

11 *Lifting arms in greeting* The baby greets his mother after separation with uplifted arms, smiles and loud shouts.

12 *Clapping hands in greeting* The baby greets his mother after separation by clapping his hands and smiling.

13 *Approach through locomotion* When the child can crawl or walk, he follows his greeting by moving towards his mother quickly, often smiling and vocalizing at the same time.

3.6 By no means all the Ganda children Ainsworth studied showed all these behaviours. Some children rarely cried, followed or clung to their mothers at the threat of separation, but did show other behaviours, such as greeting, smiling and following them with their eyes. In later work with middle-class white American children, Ainsworth, Bell and Stayton (1972) found much the same patterns of behaviours.

3.7 Not only do children vary in the sorts of behaviours they use towards attachment-figures, they also vary in the *intensity* of behaviour. Schaffer and Emerson (1964) followed the development of 60 children in the first year of life. They measured intensity of attachment by observing children's reactions to seven types of separation:

(a) When an infant was left alone in a room.

(b) When he was left with other people.

(c) When the adult passed his cot or chair without picking him up.

(d) When he was put down after being on the adult's knee.

(e) When he was put outside the house in his pram.

(f) When he was left outside the shops in his pram.

(g) When he was left in his cot at night.

3.8 In each of these situations the children's protests were ranked on a four-point scale (1 = weak protest; 4 = strong protest), and then the scores were added together to form a measure of overall attachment-intensity. Schaffer and Emerson also measured fear of strangers in a similar way by observing and rating the child's reactions to the approach of the researcher. Figure 2 shows the results of this investigation for four children.

Figure 2 The development of specific attachments and of fear of strangers in four individual infants (adapted from Schaffer, 1963).

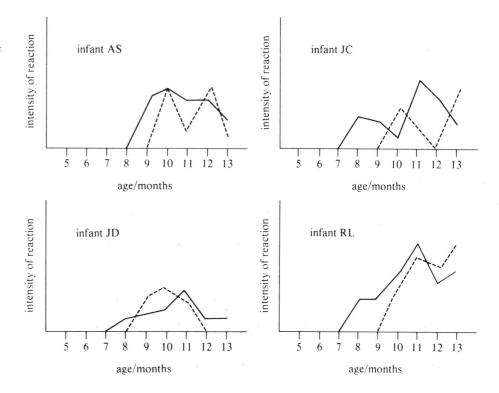

—— attachment behaviour

------ fear of strangers

15

Which of the following statements are supported by the evidence in the graphs in Figure 2?

(a) As the children become older they become more intensely attached to people about them.

(b) Some of the children are more intensely attached than others.

(c) Attachment and fear of strangers develop simultaneously.

(d) Once attachment-behaviour emerges, it tends to be a stable characteristic in individual children.

(e) The development of attachment begins from birth.

Comment

Only statement (b) is clearly supported by the evidence.

(a) In all these children, intensity of attachment fluctuates from month to month.

(b) Compare the intensity of attachment of JD and RL. What might have caused this individual variation?

(c) On the contrary, fear of strangers reliably appears one or two months later than attachment-behaviour.

(d) See comment (a).

(e) It is true to say that attachment-behaviour as Schaffer and Emerson have assessed it does not begin from birth; however, it is quite possible that other events in the first six months of life are important in determining the intensity of attachment. We shall take this up shortly.

3.9   Schaffer and Emerson found these results in the sample of 60 children. The great variation in intensity of attachment shows well that this is not an all-or-none process with a child either attached or not. Not only do attachments show themselves in many different ways, but their strength also changes over time.

Causes of attachment

3.10   One feature of the data in Figure 2 that shows very little variability in normal children is the age at which attachment–behaviour first appears, i.e. between six and eight months. This has been confirmed by several studies and has been linked to many other studies on intellectual development. The first point to note is that reactions rather similar to separation distress in response to a variety of events emerge in the second six months. For example:

(a) Children under seven months rarely show signs of fear in response to unusual events such as face masks, mechanical toy dogs and jack-in-the-boxes, but wariness increases through to 11–18 months.

(b) In one study, children began to show adverse reactions to seeing themselves in a distorting mirror only after seven months of age.

(c) If an object is repeatedly shown to infants, and then a new unfamiliar object is shown, children younger than seven or eight months usually reach for the new object immediately; older children delay slightly before reaching.

3.11   All these findings show that children do not develop wariness of unusual events and reactions to strange people and separation distress until around seven months; these reactions increase into the second year. But why?

Children older than seven months must develop in some way that allows them to show these reactions: they can do something that younger infants can't do. What conditions do you think would have to be fulfilled for infants to react to a novel unusual event?

3.12   Clearly, the child has to realize that the event is a novel one and, to do that, he has to remember what came before, hold this memory long enough to compare it with the new event, and note the discrepancy. Kagan, Kearsley and Zelazo (1978) argue that the development of *short-term memory* is the key factor in the changes mentioned

16

above. They also offer other sorts of evidence, showing how short-term memory begins to develop in the second half of the first year of life.

3.13 A study by Fox, Weiskopf and Kagan (1976) provided children with a whole range of tasks investigating memory capacity. For example:

(a) Children were given one toy to play with for 30 seconds; it was then removed for 30 seconds and given back with another new toy at the same time. Did children look back and forth between the toys before choosing one?

(b) Children were shown an object and allowed to play with it. It was then hidden under a cloth or behind a screen. Did they retrieve it?

(c) Children were shown two identical slides of smiling faces for 30 seconds; there was an interval of 30 seconds, and the children were then shown two slides, one of which was one of the previous slides, the other was a new smiling face. Did children look more at the new face than the old one?

As you can see, all these tasks require children to recall an object that is no longer visible. Fox *et al.* found that children on average first vacillated between the toys at six and a half months, retrieved an object hidden under a cloth at seven and a half months, and looked at the new slide more than the old slide at nine months. Again, we find that tasks requiring short-term recall of events emerge in the second six months of life.

Activity 9
Allow about ten minutes

The co-occurrence of so many different developments that have little else in common but a reliance on retrieval from short-term memory makes the theory of Kagan *et al.* a very plausible one, but is it a complete explanation of the growth of attachment-behaviour? Look back at the catalogue of attachment-behaviours Ainsworth provides and at the evidence in Schaffer and Emerson's study. Which pieces of evidence do not seem to involve memory, or require more than just memory to explain their occurrence?

Comment

The growth of memory may offer a partial but not a complete explanation. It gives us a good explanation of the timing of the development of attachments, but it is difficult to see how it could explain children being more prepared to explore the environment when the mother is present, or to smile, greet and make other social responses. Nor does it account for the marked individual differences in the intensity of reactions to separation seen in Figure 2.

3.14 Having discussed some of the characteristics of attachments, how they vary from child to child, and how this development is influenced by children's cognitive development, the next question is: to whom are attachments formed? Are attachments made exclusively to one person, as Bowlby contended, or to several? Are attachments made exclusively to mothers? Schaffer and Emerson examined these questions in the study I have already introduced. They found, first of all, that exclusive attachment to the mother is very rare, although in half of the children studied the most intense attachment behaviour was directed at the mother. On the other hand, one-third of the sample (at 18 months) was most attached to the father, and children who were attached to only one adult were a small percentage of the total. There was even one child whose most intense attachment was to a ten-year-old child next door. In view of these findings, the term '*maternal* deprivation' seems strange, because nearly all cases of separation involve separation from the father, siblings and other people living with the child, any of whom may play a greater role in the child's emotional life than the mother. (Compare this with the evidence in Activity 4.)

Activity 10
Allow about ten minutes

We have seen that memory explains the timing of the development of attachment behaviour, but it cannot account for the fact that attachments are only formed to some individuals, nor can it explain varying degrees of intensity of attachments. What factors might influence the formation of and intensity of particular attachments?

3.15 The important factors are likely to be found in children's experience of the people concerned, i.e. in children's social interaction with their caretakers. First of all, does the *amount* of contact between child and mother affect attachment? Kagan, Kearsley and Zelazo (1978) answered this question by comparing four different cultures that vary greatly in the degree of contact between mother and child in the first year of life. For example, on an Israeli kibbutz children are cared for by nurses in a communal nursery; parents look after children on weekdays for only one to two hours, and all day on the Sabbath. Among the !Kung San Bushmen of the Kalahari Desert contact between mother and infant is almost continual. Figure 3 shows as percentages the children studied in the four cultures who showed separation distress. There is a similar shape to the curves showing timing of growth of separation distress. However, there are marked differences in the percentage of children showing distress from 15 months onwards. Most !Kung Bushman infants show distress reactions until a much older age than others. So it seems from this data that great differences in 'mother availability' are related to the likelihood that infants will show separation distress. And, because separation distress is our primary measure of attachment, we can conclude that the amount of interaction a child experiences is related to the formation of attachments.

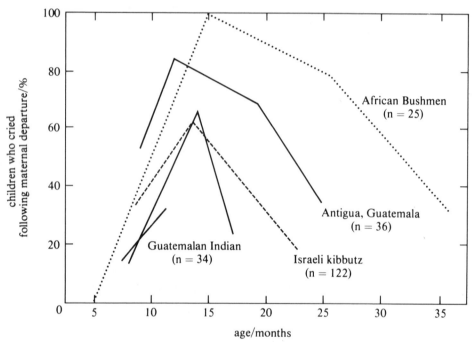

Figure 3 *Percentage of children in four different cultures who cry following maternal departure; n = number of children in sample (Kagan, Kearsley and Zelazo, 1978).*

3.16 However, it is dangerous to rely too much on limited evidence, for Kagan *et al.* also offer a comparison of distress reactions between children reared in American daycare centres while their mothers worked and children reared full-time in their own home. Here they found the percentage of children showing separation distress at five to 29 months was very similar, despite quite wide differences in the degree of contact with mothers between the two groups. This study will be further explored in Unit 5, when we shall examine evidence about the effects of day care.

Activity 11
Allow about ten minutes

What possible explanations can you offer for the difference between the results shown in Figure 3 and the American studies?

Comment First of all, although the children in the four cultures in Figure 3 differ in both amount of interaction and separation distress, the differences in separation distress are not necessarily *a result of* the amount of interaction. For example, there may be constitutional, innate differences of temperament between kibbutz and Bushman infants. Secondly, the differences, even when caused by the interaction, may not result from differences in *amount*: there are also different *patterns* of interaction, and these may account for differences in separation distress. Within one culture, it is likely that there would be fewer such differences. So the conflict in the results may

18

be more apparent than real. Thirdly, it may simply be that the differences in amount of interaction between the two American samples is not great enough to show an effect.

3.17 The amount of contact can only be the crudest measure. We need also to know about the *pattern* of the interaction between mother and child. Are particular activities important for forming attachments? Are particular patterns of interaction important? Schaffer and Emerson found that one activity which might seem important—feeding—was not associated with the formation of attachments. Many of their sample of mothers were largely responsible for feeding and yet did not become the child's primary attachment-figure. This is not to say that feeding plays no role in attachment in all mothers, for feeding may provide a context within which some mothers provide particular patterns of interaction that are important. (Compare this with what Schaffer has to say in Reading 2.1, Reader 1, under the section headed 'Mothering as physical care'.)

3.18 Schaffer and Emerson did find that two patterns of interaction in the first year of life were related to strength of attachment at eighteen months, as they measured it. The first was the readiness with which adults responded to the child's crying: the quicker an adult responded to crying the more attached the child was likely to be to that person. The second factor was the extent to which adults initiated social interactions with the child: the more an adult started social interactions with the child the more likely it was that an attachment would develop towards the adult. So both the quantity and the patterns of interaction may be important for the formation of later attachment, although it appears that, within western culture, the pattern of interaction may be more influential than its volume.

A study of early interaction and later attachment

3.19 So far we have only a crude indication of those aspects of interaction that are related to attachment, and even less information about how results in such experiments are obtained. The methods used will affect our interpretation of results, so what I want to do now is to examine in detail one study that has examined the relationship between early mother–child interaction and later attachment–behaviour. We shall look closely at both the methods of the study and at its results.

3.20 Blehar, Lieberman and Ainsworth (1977) observed a sample of 26 American middle-class white mother–infant pairs, to investigate what patterns of early interaction were associated with attachment later on. Mothers and babies were observed in their own homes on four occasions when the infants were six, nine, 12 and 15 weeks old. Each visit lasted four hours and, during this time, the observer took detailed notes of the infant's and mother's behaviour. Afterwards these notes were transcribed into a narrative account of the four-hour period. The observers were carefully briefed to pay particular attention to all face-to-face encounters between mother and infant. These narrative records were then examined and all face-to-face interactions were looked at in more detail to identify a great number of characteristics, such as who started the interaction, if there was a response, if the episode was playful. From this information many measures were recorded: these were the percentages of interactions of various kinds for each mother–child pair.

> A face-to-face encounter is defined as a full-face presentation of adult and infant to each other, occurring at a distance judged to range from 8 to 18 inches. Face-to-face episodes were coded when initiated by one member of a dyad [mother–child pair] even though the partner did not respond. They thus included instances in which (a) the baby initiated the episode by looking at a nearby person and smiling or vocalizing but received no response; (b) the adult initiated the episode by presenting his face, but the baby failed to respond; and (c) one of the dyad initiated the episode, and the other responded by at least looking . . .
>
> **Measures of maternal behavior**
>
> The following measures of maternal behavior, derived from the coding, are reported here.
>
> **Type of initiation**
>
> The percentage of mother-initiated episodes in which she initiated interactions by (a) smiling, talking or jiggling the baby or (b) merely looking at him silently and impassively.

Parent and child:
variations on a theme

Peru

Turkey

Laos

Italy

20

Korea

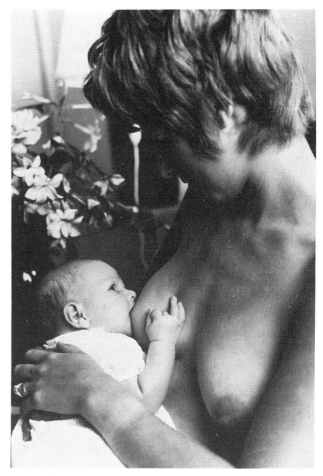

Britain

Egypt

USA

21

Presence or absence of response

The percentage of episodes in which the mother (a) responded to an infant attempt to initiate interaction or (b) did not respond or, if she herself had initiated the episode, failed to respond to any further infant social behavior.

Mother's manner during interaction

Five measures—not all mutually exclusive—reflect qualitative features of maternal behavior.

1   *Contingent pacing* The percentage of episodes in which she paced interventions slowly and gently, modifying them in keeping with infant cues, pausing if needed to allow him time to mobilize a response.

2   *Encouraging further interaction* This measure is similar to the first, in that in both the mother waits at least momentarily for a response to occur after stimulating the baby before stimulating him again. Encouragement was scored in terms of the percentage of episodes in which the mother gradually increased the intensity and/or pace of her stimulation as the baby became more responsive.

3   *Playfulness* The percentage of episodes in which the mother was playful, engaging in games (e.g. tickling games) with the baby.

4   *Routine manner* The percentage of episodes in which the mother was matter-of-fact—behavior more likely to occur during performance of routines such as changing than on non-routine occasions.

5   *Abruptness* The percentage of episodes in which the mother was rough or jerky in her interventions.

Termination of interaction

The percentage of episodes in which the mother ended the interaction by turning away, moving away, or otherwise shifting her attention from the infant—after at least having been in eye-to-eye contact with him.

Liveliness of maternal stimulation

To supplement the other measures, all of which are percentage-frequency measures, it seemed desirable to have an estimate of the general liveliness of the mother's behavior. The most feasible approach seemed to be to consider the variety of behaviors displayed by the mother in the interaction in question. On an arbitrary basis, then, a composite score was derived for each episode, by assigning one point each for a smile or for a vocalization, two points for touching the baby's face, and one additional point in any episode in which interaction continued beyond the initial stimulus–response sequence [exchange between mother and baby] . . .

Measures of infant behavior

The following measures of infant behavior were derived from the coding.

Affective state [emotional state] prior to episode The percentage of episodes in which the immediately prior state of the infant was (a) contented or neutral or (b) crying or fussing.

Initiation of interaction   The infant was judged to initiate interaction if he turned to the adult and smiled and/or vocalized. The measure is the percentage of all face-to-face episodes thus initiated.

Type of response to adult stimulation   The measures were the percentages of adult-initiated episodes in which the baby (a) smiled, (b) vocalized, (c) increased bodily activity, for example, by bouncing, (d) cried or fussed, (e) merely fixated [looked at] the adult's face, or (f) made no response.

Termination of interaction   The percentage of episodes which the infant ended by turning away from the adult or by starting to cry or fuss.

Intensity of response   Like the measure of maternal liveliness of stimulation, this measure was based on a composite of infant behaviors in a given face-to-face episode. Smiling and vocalizing were assigned one point each and bouncing two points. The intensity measure was calculated both for the initial stimulus–response sequence and for any ensuing interaction sequence. Thus the maximum possible score for an episode was 8 points.

Dyadic measures

Three additional measures depended upon both infant and adult: *Frequency of face-to-face episodes per hour; duration of interaction* (the percentage of episodes judged to be (a) brief (lasting less than 30 seconds) or (b) long (over 1 minute)); and *ensuing interaction* (the percentage of episodes in which the initial stimulus–response sequence was followed by further exchanges of smiles and/or vocalizations).

(Blehar, Lieberman and Ainsworth, 1977, pp. 185–6)

3.21   Six of the narrative records were looked at by two people working independently who identified the various characteristics described in the extract above; it was found they agreed on their descriptions of events in 84 to 96 per cent of cases.

3.22 When the children were 12 months old, they were left in a laboratory by their mothers for a few minutes. When the mother returned, observations were made of whether or not the child interacted with or made physical contact with her. This behaviour was used as the measure of security of attachment in this study, and children were classified into three groups representing degrees of strength of attachment:

Group A actively avoided contact.
Group B sought contact, closeness or interaction.
Group C were ambivalent in their reactions. They both sought and resisted contact.

Group B was further divided into three subgroups:

B1, called the 'normative group', who sought and maintained close physical contact.
B2 interacted over a distance with their mother but did not seek proximity.
B3 were like group B1, but showed these behaviours markedly less.

The authors took group B1 to be the most securely attached and groups A and C to be the least securely attached.

3.23 Let's consider the methods of this study first. The authors are taking measurements of human behaviour, and they have two different kinds of measures. Firstly, their measures of early interaction are intended only to summarize certain observations: for example, the percentage of episodes initiated by the mother is meant to indicate no more than that. They make no claims about the meaning of this figure, no statement that it indicates, say, the degree of mother-love. The measure of later attachment–behaviour is different; here they do claim that the particular behaviours they observe reflect something much broader in its scope, which covers many other behaviours, as you saw in paragraphs 3.5 to 3.8. Responses to the mother's return are an *index* of strength of attachment, much as the number of rings in a tree trunk is an index of the age of the tree.

Activity 12
Allow about ten minutes

Compare these two examples of measurements. We know that the number of rings on a tree relates directly to the age of the tree, but does the tendency to seek proximity when mother returns to the unfamiliar room directly reflect intensity of attachment? Look at the list of behaviours in paragraph 3.5. Do any contradict the definition of attachment–behaviour by Blehar *et al.*?

Comment

It isn't nearly as easy to see how to measure intensity of attachment as it is to measure age. The problem of measuring attachment is that we could argue that seeking close contact on the mother's return indicates an *insecure* attachment. Ainsworth includes in her catalogue of behaviours 'exploration from a secure base' on the grounds that securely attached children do not need as much reassurance of their mother's presence. Does this conflict with the measure of Blehar *et al.*? Could it be that group B2 are most securely attached? Or are our ideas of individual differences in attachment too crude? Perhaps we need two separate measures, one of security of attachment and one of intensity of attachment–behaviour.

3.24 Measurement of behaviour involves more than just the subject of the observation, it also involves an observer; it is important, if we are to claim that a measurement is a measurement of the subject, that it is not distorted by the observer as well. For example, to ask a Tory MP to measure the force of a Labour MP's argument is as likely to measure the Tory's political attitudes as it is to assess the Socialist's rhetoric! One way of minimizing the influence of the observer is to make the descriptions of the behaviours to be observed as clear and definite as possible, so that different observers agree on whether the behaviour has occurred.

Activity 13
Allow about ten minutes

How clear and definite are the descriptions of the following behaviours from the study by Blehar *et al.*? (Refer to the extract for the full descriptions.)

(a) Contingent pacing

(b) Playfulness

(c) Smiling (one 'type of response to adult stimulation')

(d) Termination of interaction

Comment   Behaviours (a) and (b) are rather different from (c) and (d). To take the last pair first: there is some room for disagreement about what constitutes a smile or turning away—how much turning up of the mouth is a smile, for example? Yet such behaviours are instantly recognizable by most people. There is far *more* room for disagreement in the first pair of the measures, which involve the observer in making value judgements about the subject's behaviour, evident in words like *slowly and gently* and *playful*. What counts as slow and gentle, or playful?

3.25   We can check whether or not the observer is affecting a measure of the subject's behaviour by finding out if two or more observers agree on their scoring. Blehar *et al.* have done this and found that observers agree most of the time: at least eight and a half times out of ten. But what is it they are scoring? You will see that it is not the actual behaviour but an observer's record of it, and there is no information about whether or not the observers agree on what to record. The possibility remains that the idiosyncracies of the observer have affected this narrative record.

3.26   Bearing these points in mind, let us look at the results of the study made by Blehar *et al.* You will recall that we have measures of early interaction, on which subjects differ (it would be surprising if they did not); we also have measures of security of attachment at twelve months, on which children differ. Are these two sets of differences related, so that children scoring high on some early interaction measures are more securely attached? If they are, we would have the beginnings of a case for the importance of early interaction in the formation of attachments. Blehar *et al.* investigate this relationship by comparing group B1, which they take to be most securely attached, with the two least securely attached groups, A and C. Table 1 shows the maternal and dyadic measures, and Table 2 shows the child measures. In each table the figures show percentage occurrence of the various categories of behaviour. For example, the first line of Table 1 shows that the mothers in group B1 initiated on average 9.9 per cent of interaction episodes in a silent and unsmiling manner.

Table 1 Average percentage scores of maternal and dyadic measures of early interaction for two groups varying in attachment behaviour at 12 months.

Maternal and dyadic measures	Attachment groups	
	B1	A + C
Silent unsmiling initiation	9.9	19.7
No response to baby's initiation	4.6	15.3
Contingent pacing	58.9	17.3
Encouraging further interaction	25.2	3.4
Playfulness	18.6	8.5
Routine manner	6.8	26.2
Abruptness	0.6	12.0
Liveliness of stimulation	4.9	3.7
Brief episodes	35.6	62.5
Ensuing interaction	47.3	21.1

Source: adapted from Blehar *et al.* (1977)

3.27   Table 1 shows that children in groups A and C, who either avoided their mothers or were ambivalent towards them on their return, were more likely to experience silent unsmiling mothers when their mothers started to interact with them; their mothers were less likely to respond to their opening bids for interaction and more likely to deal with them in abrupt, short and routine ways. Children in group B1, who made and kept close physical contact with their mother on her return, were more likely to have mothers who paced their behaviour to the child's behaviour, encouraged more interaction beyond the initial exchange and were playful.

3.28   Table 2 shows that children in group B1 at 12 months were more likely to smile and be physically active in interaction, and were less likely than children in groups A and C to fuss, simply look at the mother, or to end the interaction themselves.

3.29   So there are substantial differences between the two groups of children (B1 and A + C) at 12 months, related to the sort of interaction they experienced at 6–15 weeks. But how are we to interpret these results? Let's look at some possible conclusions.

Table 2 Average percentage scores of infant measures of early interaction for two groups varying in attachment behaviour at 12 months.

Infant measures	Attachment groups	
	B1	A + C
Smiling	45.0	29.5
Bouncing	21.3	5.4
Fussing	2.8	9.6
Merely looking	9.2	30.3
Baby terminates episode	11.8	26.9
Intensity of response	3.7	2.1

Source: adapted from Blehar *et al.* (1977)

Activity 14
Allow about 20 minutes

Which of the following three claims do you think are supported by the evidence in Tables 1 and 2?

(a) Face-to-face interaction of a particular type in the first three months is necessary for the development of secure attachment later on.

(b) The mother's behaviour to the child early on determines the security of attachment later.

(c) The crucial characteristics of maternal behaviours are responsiveness, sensitivity to the child's behaviour, and active warm interaction.

Comment

None of these claims is entirely satisfactory.

(a) This will not do for a number of reasons. First of all, face-to-face interaction is not the only sort possible—close contact, or a certain style of interaction during feeding might also be related to attachment. Secondly, there is no reason to suppose from these data alone that the first three months of life are any more important than the next nine. It just so happens that data are available for this period. You might well find the same relationships between three and 12 months. Thirdly, I am unsure, as I said earlier, how good a measure of secure attachment the one used here is.

(b) We cannot conclude this either, from these results alone. Although we know there is a relationship between mother's behaviour and later attachment, we do not know whether one is the cause and the other the effect. It might be that both are due to characteristics of the child: children who rarely smile and are passive in their dealings with others might lead parents to respond in a passive uninterested way, and might also be the sort of children who do not form close attachments. In fact, this study offers limited evidence that it is the mother who starts and finishes most of the interactions, and is responsible for keeping them going; but even if this were confirmed, the *quality* of the interactions could still be determined by infant or mother. As Schaffer points out in his reading, the situation is potentially even more complex than this, for a child may initially influence a mother's behaviour, which in turn may influence the child. This is an issue we shall return to later in the unit.

(c) These are the three characteristics the authors of the study use to summarize the results, and they seem reasonable enough. Responsiveness is shown to be important in the results on the measure of responses to the baby's initiation, sensitivity is indicated by the measure of 'contingent pacing' and active interaction in measures of silent, unsmiling initiation, encouraging further interaction, playfulness and liveliness of stimulation. But the wording of claim (c) is very imprecise. What does crucial mean? Does it mean these characteristics are causes? Sensitivity and responsiveness are two characteristics that we shall pick up again and analyse in more depth later on.

3.30   We can conclude, tentatively, from this study that there is a relationship between certain characteristics of face-to-face interaction in the first three months of life and children's responses to temporary separation and reunion with their mothers at 12

25

months. The characteristics which seem to show relationships involve maternal sensitivity, responsiveness and activity, and children's social and physical responsiveness.

Attachment and later development

3.31 We have established that children do become attached to adults—usually, but not always to their mother—and we have identified some of the factors that may lead to attachment-behaviours. As a study of early interaction this is interesting in its own right, but it would also be valuable to know whether the formation of attachments is important for later development.

3.32 One way to answer this question is to compare children who have formed attachments with those who have not. We might do this by comparing children who are brought up in normal family conditions with those brought up in an institutional régime that prevented the formation of attachments. Unfortunately, this would not be a good test of the hypothesis because these groups would probably differ in many more ways than in the formation of attachments. The institutionalized children may also have had less stimulation and less social contact with adults, and there would be no way of separating these factors. (Compare this with the discussion in paras. 2.3 and 2.4.)

3.33 Mia Kellmer Pringle and her colleagues made a study that avoided some of these pitfalls. They found that not all children in institutions showed signs of emotional disturbance, and when they examined the histories of these children they found that the emotionally stable children in most cases had developed attachments early in life, whereas the disturbed children had not developed attachments, and these children showed marked difficulty in making firm relationships with other people (Pringle and Bossio, 1960). Although this evidence is not strong, it does at least suggest that children who do not form attachments early in life are likely to experience emotional and social difficulties later on.

Activity 15
Allow about ten minutes

Can you suggest an alternative type of study to examine the relationship between attachment and later development, similar to the design used by Blehar *et al.*?

Comment

Pringle and Bossio study the relationship between attachment and later development in a most basic way, by comparing children who formed an attachment with those who did not. An alternative is to see if degrees of security of attachment are related to later measures of, for example, ease of forming friendships, measures of the quality of relationship with parents, social independence, etc.

Activity 16
Allow about 20 minutes

I suggest that you now summarize briefly what you have learnt so far. The following questions may help, but they are not intended to be followed strictly.

(a) What behaviours are taken to indicate attachments?

(b) How do children vary in their attachment-behaviour?

(c) To whom are attachments formed?

(d) What factors influence the timing of the development of attachment?

(e) What factors in early infancy are associated with later attachment?

(f) Is attachment important for later development?

(g) What problems are involved in observing and measuring behaviour?

---

4 Interaction in infancy

4.1   So far, I have concentrated on the role that mothers play in the emotional and social development of their children. In the debate about day care of young children, this side of things has played a very prominent part, and you will see in Unit 5 that arguments for and against providing day care have involved its supposed effects on emotional and intellectual growth. We can now look at what role parents play in the early development of their children's intellectual abilities. It should become clear that, without any explicit intentions and without any well-defined training, most parents serve a vital teaching function. Moreover, teachers rely on parents being successful in this function in order to make a success of their own job.

Reading   A great deal of interest has centred on the role that mothers play in helping their children to learn language. Catherine Snow introduces this work in her paper, 'The language of the mother–child relationship' (Reading 2.5 in Reader 1), and she raises many of the points I shall take up in the rest of the unit. Below are some questions that may guide your reading:

(a) When children learn language, they learn a lot of rules. What kinds of rules?

(b) Do infants need to be able to speak to communicate? If not, what can they use to communicate?

(c) Before the onset of language in children, how do parents communicate with their children?

(d) Does early communication between mother and child help later language development?

(e) What are the characteristics of parents' talk addressed to children between 18 months and three years old?

(f) In what ways might those characteristics help language development?

A study of direction of gaze in mothers and infants

4.2   One feature that has distinguished recent research on mother–infant communication from most work on formal schooling is the very great detail of observation. We have come to see that in order to understand how mothers influence their children we must concentrate on a limited number of particular behaviours. The behavioural analysis conducted by Blehar *et al.* takes us only part way to the very detailed analysis frequently used today. To get you used to this kind of study I would like to follow one experiment in detail.

4.3   Collis and Schaffer (1975) were interested in the extent to which mothers followed and monitored their babies' direction of gaze, and to study this they conducted very detailed analyses of videotape-recorded interactions. Their subjects were two groups of eight mother–infant pairs: in one group the children were between 19 and 27 weeks old and in the other group between 45 and 52 weeks old. Mother–infant pairs were taken into a small room, which contained no furniture apart from a chair for the mother. On one side of the room was a one-way mirror, behind which there was a video-camera. In between the window and the chair were four attractive toys—a ball, a dog, a teddy-bear and a train. Mothers were told that the experiment was to investigate what babies do in strange environments, and they were asked to be as natural and normal as possible, but to keep their baby on their knees. A timing device, which clocked units of 0.1 second, was added to the video-recording. The recording ran for six minutes from when the pair were settled in. You will notice that this set-up allowed the observers to see what the baby was looking at and what the mother was looking at.

4.4   You have already had a hint of just how very detailed the analysis of the video-recording was. The authors timed the start and finish of each look by mother and baby to the nearest tenth of a second. A look had to last longer than 0.3 seconds for it to be noted, and if someone looked away for less than 0.3 seconds and looked back at the same toy this was counted as the same look; this effectively excluded blinks from being recorded as the end of a look.

4.5 The first results this study produced were the amounts of time infants and mothers spent looking at the toys: the amount of time they spent looking at the same toy and the amount of time they spent looking at different toys. This information is given in Table 3 for each of the 16 mother–infant pairs; the last line of the table gives the average times for each column.

Table 3 Total time spent by mother and infant looking at toys and time spent looking simultaneously at same toy as opposed to different toys.

Mother–infant pair	Total time (seconds)			
	Looking at toys:		Looking simultaneously at:	
	mother	infant	same toy	different toys
Younger children:				
A1	51.5	103.1	12.3	3.2
A2	45.2	119.8	9.5	12.2
A3	11.7	82.2	4.0	0.0
A4	21.8	87.5	5.6	1.0
A5	19.5	214.2	13.9	1.7
A6	36.6	169.3	16.1	5.6
A7	83.8	175.7	19.0	13.8
A8	95.7	179.0	38.6	18.2
Older children:				
B1	17.6	94.8	8.1	0.9
B2	102.5	168.5	21.6	31.3
B3	5.2	52.4	1.9	0.0
B4	62.2	205.8	32.5	12.6
B5	57.3	138.7	25.8	13.4
B6	112.5	265.3	68.6	28.0
B7	49.0	160.5	24.1	14.0
B8	30.0	85.0	5.4	8.2
Averages	50.1	142.0	19.2	10.3

Source: adapted from Collis and Schaffer (1975)

Activity 17
Allow about five minutes

Which of the following statements are supported by the evidence presented in Table 3?

(a) If their infants spend a lot of time looking at the toys, mothers will tend to look at the toys more.

(b) Infants show considerable interest in the toys.

(c) When mother and infant are both looking at the toys, more often than not they look at different toys.

Comment

Only statement (b) is clearly supported by the evidence in Table 3.

(a) There is a relationship between the amounts of time mothers and infants look at the toys, so that the more an infant looks, the more a mother looks; but statement (a), because of its rather ambiguous wording, suggests that this is because mothers' looks are determined by their infants. No such inference can be drawn from these figures.

(b) Out of six minutes (360 seconds), children spend an average of 142 seconds looking at the toys. In an unfamiliar environment, this must mean the toys captured their interest quite successfully.

(c) Quite the reverse: more often than not mother and infant look at the *same* toy, and this is an important result we shall explore further.

4.6 We can now concentrate on the finding that mother and infant, when both looking at the toys, more often than not look at the same toy. What precisely led mother and infant to look at the same toy? Was it just chance, was the mother following what the infant did, or vice versa? Collis and Schaffer investigated this by examining the results of each mother–child pair individually. First of all they identified what the child was doing when the mother started to look at a toy, and they then identified what the mother was doing when the child started to look at a toy. The results for one pair (B4) are shown in Table 4. The boxed diagonals indicate in Table 4(a) how often the mother started to look at the toy the baby was already looking at; and in Table 4(b) the occasions when the baby started to look at the toy the mother was already looking at.

Table 4

(a) Toy at which mother started to look in relation to toy infant already looking at.					(b) Toy at which infant started to look in relation to toy mother already looking at.				
Infant looking at:	Mother started looking at:				Mother looking at:	Infant started looking at:			
	Toy 1	Toy 2	Toy 3	Toy 4		Toy 1	Toy 2	Toy 3	Toy 4
Toy 1	9	0	1	0	Toy 1	0	4	2	0
Toy 2	3	34	4	1	Toy 2	0	3	3	2
Toy 3	0	0	4	0	Toy 3	0	5	1	0
Toy 4	0	0	0	7	Toy 4	0	2	0	0
None	4	5	6	4	None	22	41	4	20

Source: Collis and Schaffer (1975)

Activity 18
Allow about ten minutes

Tables 4(a) and 4(b) allow us to make inferences about the control of one partner's direction of gaze by the other partner. What inference do you draw, particularly from a comparison of these two tables?

Comment

The mother looks at what the baby looks at far more than the reverse happens. Out of 63 mother's looks at the toys, 54 of them follow the child's gaze; when the baby is looking at one toy, very rarely does the mother look at a different toy. Table 4(b) shows that out of 22 looks at the toys by this baby only four of them follow the mother's gaze. This mother–infant pair shows this tendency to the greatest extent, but the same pattern emerges in all but two of the 16 pairs. Only in one pair is there any tendency for the baby to follow the mother's direction of gaze.

4.7 So in these conditions mothers monitor their infants' attention closely, and their attention is directed by their child's line of gaze. The child influences the mother's behaviour here, through the mother's refined sensitivity to her child's behaviour. But in what ways might this pattern of interaction be important? A clue to this comes from what Catherine Snow has to say about 'semantic restrictions'. She says that young children tend to hear language that is concerned with their everyday world, with the objects and events that surround them. The mother's ability to notice very quickly a child's line of gaze means that she can synchronize her naming and describing of objects with the child's looking at it, and thus avoid confusions where words do not match the child's current focus of attention.

4.8 Collis (1977) found that there *is* an association between infant and mother's line of gaze, and mother's naming the objects looked at. In a study of a group of infants whose ages ranged from 40 to 46 weeks old, he found that mothers were more likely to name an object when the infant was looking at it than when looking elsewhere. Thus the plausible case made above for one function of visual co-orientation is supported by observational evidence. You may recall that in paragraph 3.30 I introduced the potential significance of a mother's sensitivity to a child. This experiment provides one example of the ways in which mothers are sensitive to and adjust to what their children do. We shall encounter more examples later.

Maternal responsiveness and children's arousal

4.9   This demonstration of mothers' fine sensitivity to their infants' behaviour shows how wrong are ideas that mother–child interaction is one-way. Mothers do influence their children, but so do children influence their mothers, and Collis and Schaffer's work suggests that it is only if children influence their mothers that their mothers can in turn affect them at all. With very young babies one important characteristic that mothers must take into account is their state of arousal and alertness (often referred to simply as their *state*). Five levels of state are commonly distinguished:

1   *Deep regular sleep* eyes closed, regular breathing, no movements except startles.
2   *Active irregular sleep* eyes closed, irregular breathing, small muscular twitches, no large movements.
3   *Alert inactivity* eyes open, no large movements.
4   *Alert activity* eyes open, diffuse movements, irregular breathing.
5   *Crying* eyes partly or completely closed, vigorous diffuse movements and cries.

In the first few weeks of life, changes in the baby's state are rapid and unpredictable. Later on they become organized into rather more regular cycles of sleep and wakefulness. The important point, however, is that the baby's changes in state are partly under the control of internal mechanisms: changes can occur quite spontaneously.

4.10   The response of a baby to stimulation varies considerably with his current state, a fact which has dogged the efforts of researchers into early learning and development. Wolff (1966) studied babies' responses to slight pain, touch and sound, measuring their level of activity following these stimuli. He found that touch and sound produced most activity during irregular sleep and wakefulness (states 2, 3 and 4), but far less during regular sleep and crying. Pain, on the other hand, led to most activity during regular and irregular sleep, and less in active states. Wolff also found that the type of response made to one stimulus varied according to the baby's state—the same sound could produce smiling during irregular sleep and a startle–response during regular sleep. So, although a baby's state is partly under the control of internal mechanisms, it can also be changed by outside stimulation.

Activity 19
Allow about five minutes

What do the results of this experiment suggest to you about likely patterns of maternal behaviour in the first few weeks?

4.11   Mothers cannot ignore their babies' state when they are dealing with them; if they do, they are in danger of producing the wrong reaction altogether. You can't, say, start tickling and playing with a baby when he is in a deep sleep and expect him to respond by waking up and smiling. In fact, a study by Levy (1958) found that mothers vary their behaviour quite substantially in the way they handle, talk to and feed their babies, according to the baby's state.

4.12   However, we should not be led into oversimplified conclusions about mothers' behaviour: the facts are often more complex than we can imagine, and a study by Moss (1967) illustrates this. He observed 30 mother–infant pairs when the baby was aged three weeks and three months, and recorded measures of the baby's state and a number of maternal behaviours. He used a technique called time-sampling: for each minute of observation he recorded whether or not a particular behaviour had occurred; only one occurrence was recorded in each minute and, from these records, Moss produced scores of the number of minutes in which a behaviour had been noted. I shall focus on:

(a) *Infant behaviours*
    (i)   crying
    (ii)   fussing
    (iii) sleep

    Scores for (i) and (ii) were added together to produce a measure of irritability.

(b) *Maternal behaviours*

    (i) holds infant

    (ii) attends infant (stands close and leans over)

    (iii) maternal contact (the combined scores for 'holds' and 'attends')

    (iv) stimulates/arouses infant

4.13 Here are some of the results:

    (i) Boys were more irritable and slept less than girls at both three weeks and three months.

    (ii) At three weeks, mothers had more contact with boys and stimulated/aroused them more than girls, but there was no such difference at three months.

    (iii) More irritable girls had mothers who were in contact with them more at three weeks and at three months.

    (iv) More irritable boys were as likely to receive a lot of contact as less irritable boys at three weeks; that is, there was no relationship between irritability in boys and maternal contact at three weeks.

    (v) At three months more irritable boys were likely to receive *less* maternal contact than less irritable boys.

Activity 20
Allow about 15 minutes

Which of the following statements are supported by this evidence?

(a) Mothers respond to girls' crying and fussing by coming in contact with them.

(b) Boys are innately more irritable than girls.

(c) Crying and fussing boys receive less contact than quieter boys at three months because boys are not supposed to be spoilt.

(d) Mothers contact boys more than girls at three weeks because they are more irritable.

Comment

None of these statements can be safely concluded from the evidence.

(a) Note that the data consist of scores. It is true that more irritable girls (girls with high scores) had mothers who gave more contact, but we do not know how often the contact followed a period of crying or fussing. To begin to understand what was causing what we would need this sequential information.

(b) This may well be, because boys were more irritable at only three weeks, but it is certainly possible that even this small amount of contact with a particular caretaking style may have promoted their crying and fussing.

(c) The first part of this is correct, but the claim of a cause cannot be proved by this evidence, plausible though it may be. There is at least one equally plausible explanation, which will be discussed below.

(d) See comments (a) and (c) above.

4.14 There are many lessons to be learnt from Moss's study. First, we have found that certain factors can modify general conclusions. We concluded initially that mothers vary their behaviour to children according to their state; now we find that at three weeks this only happens with girls. At three months we continue to find that more irritable girls receive more contact, but more irritable boys receive less. Snow describes in the section 'How mothers and infants communicate' how cultural differences modify general conclusions, and of course Moss shows how age is also influential.

4.15 Secondly, relationships between global amounts of behaviour cannot tell us about sequences of behaviour. We know that more irritable girls tend to get more contact, but we don't know from Moss's evidence *when* these things happen. To claim the mother is sensitive to her child's behaviour would require information about sequences of behaviour.

4.16 To find out what causes a particular pattern of interaction involves great care in interpreting the data. Let's look at the idea that more irritable boys receive less contact than less irritable boys at three months because there is a cultural assumption that boys should not be fussed over. This doesn't work, because in fact boys as a whole receive *more* contact and stimulation than girls as a whole. Perhaps it is a cultural belief that boys should receive more active contact, but that this is to be avoided when they are crying or fussing; girls on the other hand are left to their own devices and desires, except when they make a fuss. All very plausible, but Moss has another alternative:

> Our speculation for explaining this relationship . . . is that the mothers probably were negatively reinforced for responding to a number of boys but tended to be positively reinforced for their responses towards the girls. That is, mothers of the more irritable boys may have learned that they could not be successful in quieting boys whereas the girls were more uniformly responsive to (quieted by) maternal handling.

> (Moss, 1967, p. 29)

Yet another possibility is that responsive mothers unwittingly encourage their children to cry more because babies know they will get contact if they cry. It may, of course, turn out that all three of these explanations are involved: you might have gathered this by recalling what Schaffer had to say about the 'transactional model'.

4.17 A study by Bell and Ainsworth (1972) helps to resolve part of this issue. They took similar measures of 26 mother–child pairs, every three months for the first year, and the data they present contain information about the sequence of behaviour. They measured:

(a) *Infant crying*
 (i) The frequency of crying episodes per waking hour. An episode refers to any instance of vocal protest—not always a full-blown yell.
 (ii) The duration of crying. The combined length of all crying episodes.

(b) *Maternal responsiveness*
 (i) The number of crying episodes ignored by the mother.
 (ii) Duration of unresponsiveness. How long the baby cried without the mother responding.

4.18 As with other studies in this unit, the results show very great individual differences between infants and between mothers. For example, in the first three months one baby cried 21 minutes per waking hour, another cried hardly at all; by the end of the year the range was slightly reduced, from virtually no crying to 13 minutes of crying per hour. Mothers' responsiveness was equally variable in the first three months; one mother ignored only 4 per cent of cries, another ignored 97 per cent.

4.19 Are these two variations related? In particular, Bell and Ainsworth asked if there were relationships over time. For example, do unresponsive mothers at three months tend to have babies who cry a lot later on; or do babies who cry a lot at three months tend to have unresponsive mothers later on? If these relationships over time are causal relationships (and that is a big 'if'), then the earlier factor must be the cause and the later one the effect. In fact, they found crying and responsiveness were related over time in two ways:

(a) Mothers who do not respond quickly to their babies' cries earlier on tend to have babies who cry longer later on (a finding which contrasts strongly with some beliefs about child-rearing).

(b) Babies who cry for long periods early in their first year tend to have mothers who respond slowly later on in the year.

So the relationships are two-way: mothers' unresponsiveness is associated with later crying, and babies' crying is associated with later unresponsiveness. This has the flavour of a 'vicious circle' about it, of mutual influences flowing backwards and forwards. Of course, the reverse of this rather negative way of looking at things also holds: responsive mothers have babies who cry less later on, and babies who cry less (in the second six months) have mothers who become more responsive—here is a good example of what Schaffer calls 'the constant and progressive modifications of parent and child'.

4.20 Bell and Ainsworth's study tells us about the consequences of maternal responsiveness for babies' emotional state, but are maternal responses important for other aspects of development as well? A study by Korner and Grobstein (1966) clarifies this issue. This was an experimental study: mothers themselves were not involved, because the authors wanted precise control over what happened. They were interested in what happens when crying babies are picked up and soothed, and to study this they handled in three different ways babies two to three days old who were crying. They either:

(a) left them alone;

(b) picked them up and put them to their shoulder, so providing warmth, direct contact, movement and close holding;

(c) sat them upright and held them in this position on their bed.

For 30 seconds after each handling or, in case (a), for a 30-second period, observers counted the number of times the baby opened its eyes, and the number of times the baby looked around the room. The results are shown in Table 5.

Table 5 Babies' responses to handling: percentage of trials in which eye-opening and scanning occurred.

	Type of intervention		
	None	Sat up	Picked up
Eyes opened	26	27	88
Scanning	16	15	72

Source: adapted from Korner and Grobstein (1966)

4.21   Table 5 shows that babies opened their eyes and looked around more when they were picked up and held to the shoulder than when they were either left alone or held sitting up in bed. So babies who are soothed are given more opportunity to pay attention to the environment, and this seems almost a logical precondition for learning to perceive and to understand the world. Most interesting, to me at least, is that the sort of reaction that is most often associated with the expression of love and affection towards an infant may also turn out to be of some importance for promoting a child's intellectual development. This is another illustration of how mothers act not just as a source of stimulation and interaction for their infant, but also as a means of bringing the infant to a state where he can more readily assimilate events around him. You will recall the same sort of process, but at a different age, in the study by Collis and Schaffer (1975).

Turn-taking and early communication

4.22   We have now looked at some ways in which mothers are sensitive observers of their infants and how they adjust their own behaviour to fit in with their infants' activity. This process provides the right kind of information to help babies learn. At the end of Section 4 we shall explore this further, when we look at the kind of information mothers provide for children who are learning to talk. First, we shall look at the events leading up to language.

4.23   Snow, in her section, 'How mothers and infants communicate', shows that children learn a great deal about how to communicate before they learn any words. One of the skills she describes is turn-taking, an ability that all adults possess to some degree. We have a wide variety of subtle, and sometimes not so subtle means for regulating the flow of conversations. These include cues that mean, 'I haven't stopped yet; I'm just pausing to breathe and I intend to go on', and cues that mean, 'I have stopped; you can talk now without interrupting me'. No doubt you can remember cases where you got into trouble by missing or misinterpreting these cues: 'Yes, well I—sorry, please go on!' Babies have to learn not just these cues for taking turns, but also the skill of taking turns at all. What do mothers do in the early years by way of alternating with babies and providing them with experience of turn-taking?

4.24   The first thing to note is that babies' very early behaviour, largely determined by internal mechanisms, helps a great deal. Inbuilt behaviour patterns, such as sucking, put them in immediate contact with other people. Sucking is not just a stereotyped response to an object thrust into a baby's mouth, but a highly organized and adaptable system of responses. An important aspect of this organization is the burst–pause pattern. Sucking occurs in sequences of bursts of sucks and pauses, and this rhythm offers the key to one of the child's first experiences of taking turns. Kenneth Kaye has conducted detailed analyses of mothers feeding their babies (either by bottle or breast) to see whether mothers alternate their behaviour with their babies (Kaye, 1977). He and his co-workers observed mothers and babies at two days and two weeks after birth, and recorded the babies' sucking and the mothers' 'jiggling', i.e. moving the baby's body or cheek, the breast or the bottle. He found that when the baby was sucking, mothers were much less likely to jiggle him, and when he stopped sucking they were more likely to jiggle him. Contrary to the mothers' firm belief that jiggling encouraged the baby to start sucking, it actually tended to prolong pauses between bursts. What actually happened was that the *end* of a jiggle increased the likelihood of a burst of sucks. This pattern, whether or not mothers were aware of it, obviously affected their behaviour. Between two days and two weeks, mothers reduced the length of their jiggling so the pattern became more 'jiggle and stop' rather than 'jiggle until he starts sucking'. Yet again, we see that *sensitivity* to the baby is at the centre of things. The fact that mothers and babies alternate their behaviour even two days after birth is due largely to the way the mother fits in with the baby's internally regulated rhythm of bursts and pauses. The mother very quickly, indeed almost unconsciously, tunes in to her baby's responses and modifies her own behaviour accordingly. So the first social exchanges begin.

4.25 Snow offers some examples of 'proto-conversations' to show how turn-taking develops in slightly older children. But what evidence can we marshal here? How smoothly do mothers and infants manage to run their communication with each other? To answer this question, Schaffer, Collis and Parsons (1977) videotaped mothers with one-year-old and two-year-old children playing together with a variety of toys. Each play session lasted ten minutes and a timer which clocked in 0.1 second units was added to the videotape record. Schaffer *et al.* noted the timing of every instance of vocal behaviour by mother and child. This included every vocal noise, except coughs and sneezes. It covered much more than just words, so here I shall refer to 'vocalizing' rather than 'speaking'. They also noted the timing of every look by one partner at the other.

4.26 They found that overlaps, when the two partners were vocalizing together, were very rare—only an average of 11 overlaps in the younger group and 12 in the older group. Overlaps that did occur were generally very short, many less than one second, and only very momentarily upset the dialogue. Mothers were as likely as children to cause the problem. Of course, not all overlaps are problems: many are perfectly normal examples of laughing together, or chorusing, or cases where the mother soothes an upset child, so, when these are subtracted from the figures above, the dialogue appears even smoother.

4.27 Mothers also appear to be very good at following their child's vocalization quickly: pauses in between a child's and his mother's vocalization were mostly very short, with only 25 per cent longer than one second. Children, on the other hand, took much longer to follow their mothers. So here again we have evidence of mothers' considerable sensitivity to their children. But what is the basis for this sensitivity? How do they manage to respond so quickly and at the same time avoid interrupting their children? The actual language spoken by the children is likely to be of little help, especially with the one-year-olds, because at this age most children use only short distinct utterances, which are often not closely connected to each other, so it is often difficult to tell whether an utterance is likely to be followed by another. Nor can the children's intonation be a great help at this age, because their grasp of adult forms of intonation is quite limited. Mothers may well have picked up much useful information by watching their child, because we can assume that there is some relationship between what children say and what they do. In fact, Schaffer *et al.* found that mothers spent a great deal of time looking at their children—an average of 90 per cent of the observed time—and so they were in a good position to monitor their children's behaviour very closely. It is worth noting that the pattern of children's looks at their mothers is very different: the one-year-olds looked at their mother only 5 per cent of the time and the two-year-olds 12 per cent of the time. These figures give a strong impression of mothers, in this situation, allowing children to dictate the overall pattern of the session but following them very closely indeed and ensuring that their vocal interchange occurs smoothly. Later, as children begin to learn more of the rules for speaking and listening, they can take a greater part in regulating the dialogue, but precisely when and how this happens is not known at present.

Maternal speech and children's language acquisition

4.28 Learning to take turns is just the beginning of learning to talk: this process gets under way in earnest at around 18 months. We can now look at the role mothers play in helping their children to this most dazzling of early achievements. Snow gives a lot of information about the ways mothers' speech to young children is different from adult-addressed speech: in the sound patterns, intonation, meaning and grammatical structure. It is rather easy to assume that these differences actually help children to learn to talk, because we often see mothers dealing with children in a distinctly different way from the way they deal with adults. In fact, this kind of assumption isn't always warranted. Take 'baby-talk': does saying 'bow-wow' and 'go bye-byes' actually make language any clearer for children, or does it serve only to confuse even further? Does speaking in short sentences help? Does repetition help?

Activity 21
Allow about 15 minutes

Catherine Snow makes some statements about the functions of mothers' speech styles. Look back at Snow (from 'How mothers talk to children' to the end) and note down:

(a) what she claims are the reasons why mothers speak as they do to their children;

(b) what she claims are the results of this speech style.

Comment

The reasons for mothers' speech style and the results of this style are rather different. According to Snow, mothers do not consciously alter their speech because they believe that simplified language helps a child to learn to talk. The style arises partly from the contingencies of communicating with an immature speaker. In order for a mother to make herself understood she must simplify both the meaning and form of her language. If the language is of the wrong kind, Snow claims that it may be ignored or met with other signs of non-comprehension. However, this does not adequately explain certain features such as high pitch, consonant cluster simplification and syllable reduplication. Why these have arisen in so many and diverse cultures is very puzzling.

Snow is very careful about the claims she makes about the consequences of mothers' speech for children's development. She makes out plausible cases for the importance of mothers' speech in connection with the theory of semantic primacy and the repetition of sentences, but she does not claim categorically that mothers' speech is of positive benefit for children learning language.

4.29 The crucial experiment that would allow us to determine the importance of mothers' speech style simply cannot be done. There are overwhelming ethical objections to exposing children to adult styles of language in order to compare them with children who hear mothers' speech style. This leaves us with the kind of investigation used by Blehar *et al.* (1977) and Bell and Ainsworth (1972), in which relationships between variations in mothers' speech and variations in child language later on are investigated. For example, do mothers who use more short sentences that describe the 'here and now' environment around the child have children who develop language faster? In order to answer this sort of question we need to follow a group of children from the time they begin to learn language to the time when they are becoming more sophisticated speakers, making observations of their mothers' speech at the early stages, and relating it to measures of their language development later. In fact, relatively few studies of this kind have been made, so what we know about the actual effects of mothers' speech is rather limited.

4.30 One study that provides some information about the effects of mothers' speech was carried out by Newport, Gleitman and Gleitman (1977). They studied a group of children aged from 12 months to 32 months; they made recordings of mothers' and children's language at two successive ages, and produced several measures of the mothers' speech style and the children's rate of language development.

4.31 One well-established aspect of mothers' speech that Snow describes is the much shorter utterances used, and it would be a reasonable guess that this helps children by restricting the information they have to take in. Newport *et al.* looked to see if there were any effects on a range of measures of language development. These included the average length of children's utterances, the average number of verbs and nouns per utterance, how many inflections and auxiliary verbs the children used. (*Inflections* are elements like the –s on the end of a word to make it plural, or the –'s to make a possessive like 'John's'. *Auxiliary verbs* are verbs like 'can', 'will', 'do', 'must', 'could', in 'I *can* work till midnight', 'I *will* finish this unit', 'I *could* have a cup of coffee instead'.) All these measures increase in the second two years of life as children get older.

4.32　All these measures failed to show that children who heard shorter, or indeed longer, utterances early on learnt language any faster. And, in contrast to Snow's suggestion, Newport *et al.* found that mothers who repeated themselves a lot tended to have children who developed language at a *slower* rate. So a difference between speech addressed to adults and to children doesn't guarantee any effects, positive or negative, on the children's language development.

4.33　However, the research done by Newport *et al.* did show up some rather more detailed, unfamiliar and at first sight curious relationships. A marked relationship was found between the frequency with which mothers asked questions requiring yes–no answers (such as 'Are you coming?') and their children's development of the use of auxiliary verbs. Why should this be? The first clue that this might be more than a chance relationship is that yes–no questions very often begin with an auxiliary: '*Can* you find it?', '*Are* you feeling all right?', '*Do* you see?' The necessary link is provided by evidence that children tend to pay particular attention to the beginning of utterances, so there seems a good chance they might learn parts of speech faster that occur in this position. So the children's growing use of auxiliary verbs is strongly related to the mother's tendency to use these at the beginning of utterances. More support for this theory is that the child's use of the auxiliary is not at all influenced by the mother's use of questions such as 'What can you see?' and 'Where are you going?', in which the auxiliary verb comes second.

4.34　Thus it appears that specific features of mothers' language show specific relationships with children's language development, and general conclusions such as 'mothers' simple language helps their children learn language' are at best gross generalizations, at worst plain misleading.

4.35　A final point concerns a general drawback in this kind of study. It is that the relationships found between variation in mothers' speech and variation in children's language development cannot be interpreted straightforwardly as one of cause and effect. We cannot automatically claim that the mother's use of yes–no questions leads to the child's development of auxiliary verbs, for it may be that something else, which goes hand-in-hand with the use of yes–no questions, is the causal factor. A more obvious example may help here. I do not have evidence to prove this, but I suspect there is probably a fairly strong relationship between the size of a family's garden and the size of their car: the bigger the garden, the bigger the car. It is immediately clear that, although these two may be related, no one would argue that having a big garden caused you to have a big car, or vice versa. And without too much extra effort we can work out that both things are related—causally related in this case—to how rich the family is. The important difference between this banal example and the complex relationships Newport *et al.* have established is that we know a lot about money, gardens and cars but rather less about mothers' speech, but our relative ignorance should not, dare I say it, lead us up the garden path.

4.36　We have seen ways in which mothers are *sensitive* to their children's behaviour and abilities, e.g. in the way they can follow a baby's direction of gaze; we have seen how mothers *adjust* their behaviour to children, e.g. in the way they talk in shorter, simpler sentences, and we have seen how mothers provide the experiences on which children build basic human capacities. To this must be added the warning not to assume that mothers' behaviour to children is necessarily beneficial to the children's development, and the further warning not to assume that relationships established between mothers' behaviour and child development are necessarily cause–effect relationships.

Activity 22
Allow about 20 minutes

As we are at the end of a section, I suggest you stop and briefly revise Section 4. You may find the following questions helpful:

(a)　What aspects of babies' behaviour affect their earliest social relationships?

(b)　In what ways are mothers sensitive to their infants?

(c) In what ways is a mother's responsiveness to her baby important?

(d) What functions does the mother serve in her child's early social and intellectual development?

---

5 Summary and conclusions

5.1 This unit began with the educational issue: what claims to expertise do teachers have in the education of children? We have come a long way from that question and gone through several research studies in detail, so it is as well to summarize what has been learnt. Above all, it should be clear now that parents play a vital role in children's development. This is not to say that people who are not parents could not play this role—that is an issue for Unit 5. I have concentrated on the abilities that schools tend to take for granted, except when things go badly wrong, such as emotional development and language. It is because most children are emotionally stable and linguistically competent that we often assume that these things 'happen naturally' without too much fuss. They *do* happen naturally, but they are no less complex and marvellous for that. This unit has only just scratched the surface in trying to unravel how parents help children to grow up.

5.2 Let's summarize the topics we have surveyed. First of all, we looked at what we can discover about mothers' roles through the investigation of children deprived of normal mothering. Do these children develop differently? We found that children placed in institutions can be affected adversely in both their emotional and intellectual development. However, it became clear that many factors affected children's responses: what matters are the kinds of experiences children have in institutions, not the fact that they are placed in an institution as such. Investigation of the factors that modify children's responses can tell us about those aspects of normal experience that may be important for children's development.

5.3 Next, we explored the beginnings of the emotional relationship between mother and child, and how the mother's behaviour to the child can influence this. We concentrated on the formation of attachment bonds. This abstract idea is revealed in a variety of behaviours; children vary considerably in how intense their attachments to people are, and mothers are by no means the only people to whom attachments are formed. We found that emotional development and intellectual growth are related through the development of short-term memory, but memory is only one cause in a complex of factors that influence attachment formation. There is evidence that both the quantity and patterns of interaction that children experience affect attachment, but in the detailed analysis of the study by Blehar *et al.* it became clear how difficult it is to establish precise links.

5.4 In Section 4 we looked at intellectual development and concentrated on language and the skills that precede language. We saw that mothers' very refined capacity to observe their infant's activity allowed them to adapt their behaviour to match that of their child. This was illustrated in their ability to follow infants' line of gaze, to take account of babies' level of arousal, to adapt to babies' feeding patterns, and to take account of linguistic immaturity. As with other topics, the study of Moss showed how generalized conclusions about mother–child interaction can be refined and modified by a variety of factors. Finally, we looked at the problems involved in trying to show that what mothers do actually has an effect on their children. Obviously the overall effect cannot be denied, but the detailed mechanisms through which mothers influence their children remain very clouded.

5.5 In conclusion, you might think about two issues. First, how much do teachers and parents have in common in the ways they educate children? Are teachers sensitive to their pupils' abilities? Do they adapt their behaviour to suit particular children? How much effect do they have on their pupils? You should not take these questions to imply that all parents are sensitive and adapt ideally to their children, or that all teachers are insensitive. But I think that the composition of the two roles may be more similar than we often recognize. Secondly, who knows most about children? Their parents? Their teachers? Does it make sense for children to start school at five with adults they do not know who often have had or will have only the very slightest opportunity to talk to parents about their children. How far should parents be involved in classrooms, in interacting with their children to achieve specific aims? Is the cultural divide we maintain between home and school a rational one?

References

AINSWORTH, M. D. S. (1964) 'Patterns of attachment behavior shown by the infant in interaction with his mother', *Merrill-Palmer Quarterly*, **10**, pp. 51–8.

AINSWORTH, M. D. S. and BELL, S. M. (1970) 'Attachment, exploration and separation: illustrated by the behavior of one-year-olds in a strange situation', *Child Development*, **41**, pp. 49–67.

AINSWORTH, M. D. S. and STAYTON, D. J. (1972) 'Individual differences in the development of some attachment behaviors', *Merrill-Palmer Quarterly*, **18**, pp. 123–43.

BAERS, M. (1954) 'Women workers and home responsibilities', *International Labour Review*, **69**, pp. 338–55.

BELL, S. M. and AINSWORTH, M. D. S. (1972) 'Infant crying and maternal responsiveness', *Child Development*, **43**, pp. 1171–90.

BLEHAR, M. C., LIEBERMAN, A. F. and AINSWORTH, M. D. S. (1977) 'Early face-to-face interaction and its relation to later mother–infant attachment', *Child Development*, **48**, pp. 182–94.

BOWLBY, J. (1953) *Child Care and the Growth of Love*, Harmondsworth, Penguin Books.

BOWLBY, J. (1969) *Attachment and Loss: vol. 1 Attachment*, London, The Hogarth Press.

COLLIS, G. M. (1977) 'Visual co-orientation and maternal language' in SCHAFFER, H. R. (ed.) *Studies in Mother–Infant Interaction*, London, Academic Press.

COLLIS, G. M. and SCHAFFER, H. R. (1975) 'Synchronization of visual attention in mother–infant pairs', *Journal of Child Psychology and Psychiatry*, **16**, pp. 315–20.

DENNIS, W. (1960) 'Causes of retardation among institutional children: Iran', *Journal of Genetic Psychology*, **96**, pp. 47–59.

FOX, N., WEISKOPF, S. and KAGAN, J. (1976) 'The influence of memory in stage IV object permanence'. Unpublished manuscript.

GOLDFARB, W. (1955) 'Emotional and intellectual consequences of psychological deprivation in infancy: a re-evaluation' in HOCH, P. H. and ZUBIN, J. (eds) *Psychopathology of Childhood*, New York, Grune and Stratton.

HARLOW, H. F. and HARLOW, M. K. (1969) 'Effects of various mother–infant relationships on rhesus monkey behaviours' in FOSS, B. M. (ed.) *Determinants of Infant Behaviour*, **4**, London, Methuen.

KAGAN, J., KEARSLEY, R. B. and ZELAZO, P. R. (1978) *Infancy: its place in human development*, Harvard, Harvard University Press.

KAYE, K. (1977) 'Towards the origin of dialogue' in SCHAFFER, H. R. (ed.) *Studies in Mother–Infant Interaction*, London, Academic Press.

KORNER, A. F. and GROBSTEIN, R. (1966) 'Visual alertness as related to soothing in neonates: implications for maternal stimulation and early deprivation', *Child Development*, **37**, pp. 867–76.

LEVY, D. M. (1958) *Behavioral Analysis*, Springfield, Illinois, Thomas.

MOSS, H. A. (1967) 'Sex, age and state as determinants of mother–infant interactions', *Merrill-Palmer Quarterly*, **13**, pp. 19–36.

NEWPORT, E. L., GLEITMAN, H. and GLEITMAN, L. R. (1977) 'Mother, I'd rather do it myself: some effects and non-effects of maternal speech style' in SNOW, C. E. and FERGUSON, C. A. (eds) *Talking to Children: language input and acquisition*, Cambridge, Cambridge University Press.

THE OPEN UNIVERSITY (1976) E201, *Personality and Learning*, Milton Keynes, The Open University Press.

THE OPEN UNIVERSITY (1979) E362, *Cognitive Development*, Milton Keynes, The Open University Press.

PRINGLE, M. K. and BOSSIO, V. (1960) 'Early prolonged separations and emotional adjustments', *Journal of Child Psychology and Psychiatry*, **1**, pp. 37–48.

PROVENCE, S. and LIPTON, R. C. (1962) *Infants in Institutions*, New York, International Universities Press.

ROBERTSON, J. and BOWLBY, J.(1952) 'Responses of young children to separation from their mothers', *Courrier du Centre International de l'Enfance*, **2**, pp. 131–42.

SAYEGH, Y. and DENNIS, W. (1965) 'The effect of supplementary experiences upon the behavioral development of infants in institutions', *Child Development*, **36**, pp. 81–90.

SCHAFFER, H. R. (1963) 'Some issues for research in the study of attachment behaviour' in FOSS, B. M. (ed.) *Determinants of Infant Behaviour II*, London, Methuen.

SCHAFFER, H. R., COLLIS, G. M. and PARSONS, G. (1977) 'Vocal interchange and visual regard in verbal and preverbal children' in SCHAFFER, H. R. (ed.) *Studies in Mother–Infant Interaction*, London, Academic Press.

SCHAFFER, H. R. and EMERSON, P. E. (1964) 'The development of social attachments in infancy', *Monographs of the Society for Research in Child Development*, **29**, (94).

WOLFF, P. H. (1966) *The Causes, Controls and Organization of Behavior in the Neonate*, New York, International Universities Press.

WORLD HEALTH ORGANIZATION (1951) *Expert Committee on Mental Health, Report on the Second Session*, Technical Report Series No. 31, Geneva: World Health Organization.

Acknowledgements

Grateful acknowledgement is made to the following for permission to reproduce material in this unit:

Text

M. C. Blehar *et al.* (1977) 'Early face-to-face interaction and its relation to later mother–infant attachment', *Child Development*, **48,** University of Chicago Press.

Tables

Tables 3 and 4 from G. M. Collis and H. R. Schaffer (1975) 'Synchronization of visual attention in mother–infant pairs', *Journal of Child Psychology and Psychiatry*, **16** (242), Pergamon Press Ltd.

Figures

Figure 2 from B. M. Foss (ed.) (1963) *Determinants of Infant Behaviour*, Methuen. Reprinted by permission of the Tavistock Institute of Human Relations; *Figure 3* from J. Kagan *et al.* (1978) *Infancy: its place in human development*, Harvard University Press. Copyright © 1978 by the President and Fellows of Harvard College.

Illustrations

p. 20 (top) Giles Marking; *p. 20 (centre left, centre right and bottom)* Keystone Press; *p. 21 (top left, centre left and bottom)* Keystone Press; *p. 21 (top right)* Camera Press/Claire Wright.

E200 Contemporary Issues in Education

Block 1   Introductions
Unit 1   Education through autobiography
Unit 2   Questions about education

Block 2   The family as educator: the childhood years
Unit 3   Learning in the family
Unit 4   Mother–child interaction
Unit 5   Day care outside the family
Unit 6   Parents and teachers

Block 3   Control and choice in education
Unit 7   Teaching institutions
Unit 8   Institutions of educational government
Unit 9   Who should control the curriculum?
Unit 10   Control and choice in the school
Unit 11   Responding to falling school rolls
Unit 12   Post-secondary education: access and control
Unit 13   Education and social change
Unit 14   William Tyndale: the system under stress

Block 4   Educational standards
Unit 15   Teaching styles
Unit 16   Education and equality
Unit 17   Schools and deviance
Unit 18/19   Examinations and assessment
Unit 20   Certification, education and work

Block 5   The family as educator: adult life
Unit 21   Personal change in adults
Unit 22   Marriage and parenthood
Unit 23   The family and later life

Block 6   Work, leisure and learning
Unit 24   Careers and work cultures
Unit 25   The division of labour by gender
Unit 26   Leisure, work and education

Block 7   Education and the future
Unit 27   Introducing the future
Unit 28   Visions of the future
Unit 29   Computers, communication and learning
Unit 30   The future of educational institutions
Unit 31   The costs of education

Block 8   Review
Unit 32   What is education?